Brigh
Gra

An English Grammar with Exercises

BOOK THREE
New Edition

Phebean Ogundipe
C. E. Eckersley
Margaret Macaulay

LONGMAN

Pearson Education Limited,
Edinburgh Gate, Harlow,
Essex CM20 2JE, England
and Associated Companies throughout the world.

First published 1953
New edition 1983
Twenty-ninth impression 2009

Set in 10/12 Helvetica

Printed in Malaysia, LSP

ISBN 978-0-582-60973-0

Preface

This is a new edition of *Brighter Grammar*. The continued popularity of this book, over the years, has shown that the necessity of grammar in the learning of a language is appreciated, not only by curriculum planners and teachers of English, but also by the students. School students like to have a handy revision book to reinforce lessons. Private students need a clear yet concise course to bring their competence in English to the level required, either to facilitate their further studies in professional fields, or for increased efficiency at their work places.

The success of *Brighter Grammar* has been due firstly to the fact that the subject is made completely understandable to even the least linguistically-minded student, by presenting it as simply and as clearly as possible. In the course only the essentials of grammar have been chosen, and these have been explained with the minimum of technical terms. Only those terms are taught which are necessary to understand the structure of the language and to aid the student's progress in all essential aspects, including composition.

Secondly, to show that the learning of grammar can be as enjoyable as that of any subject in the curriculum, the books have been made as lively and amusing as possible. Stories have been used as material for exercises and for 'report' work in the composition lessons. The sentences in the exercises have been made as 'real' as possible, and the four books brightened by lively drawings.

In addition, special attention has been paid to the exercises, which are graded, and nothing is asked of the student that he cannot answer from the lesson on which the exercise is based. Also, wherever necessary, the lessons in Book 2, Book 3 and Book 4 are preceded by a revision of the work covered in the earlier book or books.

This new edition will make *Brighter Grammar* even more useful than before. The course has been completely revised, and the improvements fall into three major categories:

1   Greater relevance to the African scene by the modification or even removal of culturally distant examples and stories, replacing them with usages, examples and stories more familiar to the African student.

2   Up-dating and modernising of the linguistic material to take into account the changes of idiom and usage which have made obsolete, or at least antiquated, certain items in the original edition. This up-dating is even more important to the African student than the editing or removal of references to a foreign culture. Any alert African student of English is aware that he is likely to come across references to a culture different from his own, and is therefore prepared to recognise and make efforts to understand them. But if periodic up-dating is not done, the student may find himself carefully learning some idiom or usage which, when used, will sound odd or outlandish to a contemporary native English speaker.

3   Occasional expansion or analysis of some grammatical points, so as to supply information which the original edition apparently assumed to be already known to the student. This filling in of gaps will be helpful to every student, especially those using the books on their own outside a classroom situation.

The authors therefore hope that *Brighter Grammar*, in this new and improved form, will continue to aid students, and give some relief to overburdened teachers, for many years to come.

Phebean Ogundipe
Lagos, Nigeria

Contents

1 Pronouns

Revision (from Book 1). Pronouns are words that stand instead of nouns. Personal pronouns are pronouns that stand instead of the names of people. They can be singular number or plural number, masculine gender or feminine gender. *It* is an impersonal pronoun, neuter gender. A pronoun may be in the nominative case or the objective case. The nominative form of many pronouns is different from their objective form. In this, pronouns are not like nouns.

Reflexive Pronouns

Let's look in that Pronoun box again and see if there are any more pronouns. Yes, here are three or four more. Let's look at this one first, the one which is saying '... self' '... self'.

It always ends in *– self* (or *– selves* for the plural). It appears as *myself, yourself, himself, herself, itself, oneself, ourselves, yourselves, themselves.*

Let us see some of these pronouns at work.

I saw *myself* in the mirror.

Be careful or you will hurt *yourself*.

Hamzat helped *himself* to the cakes.

Mary dressed *herself* carefully for the party.

One must be allowed to please *oneself*.

The kitten can now feed *itself*.

We taught *ourselves* to swim.

The boys hurt *themselves* getting over the wall.

There is, of course, a difference in meaning between:

'Timi hit *him*' and 'Timi hit *himself*.'

In the '-self' sentences, **the subject of the sentence is the same person or thing as the object of the sentence**. The action doesn't go from one person to another. It comes back again – like the reflection in a mirror – to the doer of the action. These '–self' pronouns are called **Reflexive Pronouns**.

The wrong use of some reflexive pronouns can lead to very odd sentences: e.g.

Now that we have met ourselves . . .

Have you two saluted yourselves?

Friends should help themselves.

In the first two cases, the speaker has said an impossible thing – you can meet or salute someone else, but you cannot meet yourself, and if you salute yourself people will think you are mad! In the third case, it is possible to help yourself, but this is not what the speaker wants to say, he wants to say that a friend should help another friend. What we need in the three cases, and in similar cases, is 'each other' or 'one another': e.g.

Now that we have met each other . . .

Have you two saluted each other?

Friends should help one another.

Emphasizing Pronouns

But this is not the only work that the '–self' pronouns do. Look at these sentences:

George bathed *himself*. I know he did, I saw him, *myself*.

You, *yourself*, said he looked clean and George, *himself*, said he had had a bath.

The first *himself* is quite plainly a reflexive pronoun; the subject George and the object *himself*, both stand for the same boy. Both are needed for a complete sentence. But the others are different. They could be missed out and the sentences would still make sense. They are put in the sentence to make what is said stronger, to make it more emphatic, and so they are called **Emphasizing Pronouns.**

Emphasizing pronouns sometimes have the meaning of 'alone', in which case they often have 'by' with them, e.g.

I went there all by *myself*.

This is an engine that goes by *itself*.

George made that model aeroplane all by *himself*.

Here are the –*self* pronouns (reflexive and emphasizing) arranged in a table.

	Singular	Plural
1st person	myself	ourselves
2nd person	yourself	yourselves
3rd person	himself	themselves
	herself	
	itself	
	oneself	

Exercises

A Put reflexive pronouns into the blank spaces:

    1 Father cut _____ when he was shaving.

    2 Mary saw _____ in the mirror.

    3 We saw _____ in the mirror.

    4 I taught _____ to play the piano.

    5 The kitten tried to bite me, and bit _____ by mistake.

    6 One can easily lose _____ in the forest.

    7 We injured _____ while playing football.

    8 If you would like some cakes, children, help _____.

    9 Heaven helps those who help _____.

    10 There are plenty of cakes here, Rufai, help _____.

B Put emphasizing pronouns into the blank spaces:

    1 He did the work all by _____.

    2 I saw him do it _____.

    3 Mary sewed those dresses _____.

4 One can't lift a heavy weight like that by _____.

5 You children must tidy this room _____. I am not going to help you.

6 The children tidied the room by _____.

7 Do you think, Mary, that you can cook the dinner by _____ today?

8 We cooked the dinner entirely by _____.

9 This machine works by _____.

10 You and Peter can do that job by _____.

C Say whether the words in italics are reflexive pronouns or emphasizing pronouns. Give reasons for your answers:

1 I have burnt *myself*.

2 Just look at *yourself* in the mirror!

3 Did you make that dress *yourself*?

4 Yes, I made it all by *myself*.

5 Did Mary teach *herself* to sew?

6 Yes, she learned all by *herself*.

7 The headmaster *himself* caned Daju.

8 He said he had enjoyed *himself*.

9 Last year's prefects made *themselves* very unpopular.

10 They *themselves* were to blame for that.

2 Pronouns (2)

Possessive Pronouns

Now let us have a look at this fellow, the possessive pronoun. I want you to go back for a moment to the lessons on adjectives. (Book 2, Lessons 4 and 5) You will remember that we had adjectives that showed possession.

My book, *your* cat, *his* dog, *her* flowers, *our* house, *their* garden.

But in the following sentences there are some other words that show possession:

That book is *mine*.

That seat isn't *yours*.

Lend me your bicycle; *hers* is no good.

He's wearing a hat that isn't *his*.

That cat is *ours*.

We spent Christmas day with the Nwosus. *Theirs* was the best party I have ever been to.

The words *yours*, *mine*, *ours*, etc., don't qualify nouns. They show possession, and here they are standing instead of nouns; *yours* means, in that sentence, 'your seat', *hers* means 'her bicycle'. They are **Possessive Pronouns**.

You will quite often find the possessive pronouns used with 'of', like this:

He is a friend *of mine*.

Is that boy a cousin *of yours*?

Not 'a friend of me' as you might expect.

Here are one or two other examples:

That dog *of yours* has been fighting again.

There's John and that friend *of his*, going to play football.

On the next page there is a table, so that you can compare the possessive pronouns and the possessive adjectives.

Possessive Adjectives	Possessive Pronouns
This book is *my* book.	This book is *mine*.
This book is *your* book.	This book is *yours*.
This book is *his* book.	This book is *his*.
This book is *her* book.	This book is *hers*.
This book is *our* book.	This book is *ours*.
This book is *their* book.	This book is *theirs*.

Pronouns that show possession are Possessive Pronouns.

Interrogative Pronouns

There are some pronouns that we use when we ask questions, e.g.

Who are you?

What have you done today?

Which of these books do you want?

Pronouns that are used to ask questions are Interrogative Pronouns.

Demonstrative Pronouns

Here are four pronouns whose work is to point out things.

This is a book.	*These* are my books.
That is a star.	*Those* are stars.

Pronouns that 'point out' are called Demonstrative Pronouns.

RUFAI   Please, sir, you told us that *this* and *that*, *these* and *those*, *what* and *which*, were adjectives. (*Book 1, Chapter 8*)

TEACHER   I did.

RUFAI   But now you say they are pronouns.

TEACHER   Rufai, read me the 'rule' on page 2 of Book 2.

RUFAI (*reads*)   'You tell what part of speech a word is by the work it does.'

TEACHER   Right. Now look at these sentences:

A	B
Which book do you want?	*Which* of these books do you want?
What exercises have you done today?	*What* have you done today?
This book is a good one.	*This* is a good book.

That star is called Mars.

These books belong to the teacher.

Those stars are millions of miles away.

That is a very bright star.

These are the teacher's books.

Those are very distant stars.

In column A, *which, what, this, that, these, those* are adjectives because they go with nouns. In column B, they are pronouns because they stand instead of nouns. They are subjects of a sentence just as nouns often are. Is that all clear now, Rufai?

RUFAI   Yes, sir. I understand it now.

Exercises

A Put possessive pronouns in the blank spaces:
  1 I own that cat; that cat is _____.
  2 You own that cat; that cat is _____.
  3 He owns that cat; that cat is _____.
  4 She owns that cat; that cat is _____.
  5 They own that cat; that cat is _____.

B In the following sentences use the verb *to be* instead of the verb *belong*. Make any other necessary changes:
  For example: That house belongs to me.
               That house is mine.

1 Those shoes belong to her.
2 That new house belongs to him.
3 These shoes belong to you.
4 That picture belongs to me.
5 That car belongs to us.
6 Those flowers belong to them.
7 Does that cat belong to you?
8 Do those toys belong to her?
9 Do these chocolates belong to us?
10 Did those chocolates belong to them?

C Put in the missing possessive adjectives and possessive pronouns.

1 I've eaten all _____ bread, can I have some of _____ ?
2 Tell Hassan not to forget _____ book. And you mustn't forget _____.
3 George has lost _____ pen. Ask Mary if she will lend him _____.
4 We've had _____ dinner; have they had _____?
5 Sam has a dog and so have I. _____ dog and _____ had a fight.
6 Have you heard from that friend of _____ who went to Lagos?
7 The teacher wants you to return that book of _____ that he lent you.
8 Miama wants to know if you've seen a pair of shoes of _____.
9 Mr and Mrs Dina and a friend of _____ are coming to see us.
10 We are going to Paris to stay with a French friend of _____.
11 Dinner has been ready a long time. I have had _____ and Mary has had _____; come and have _____.

D Make two sentences containing *which* as an interrogative pronoun, two containing *which* as an interrogative adjective; two containing *that* as a demonstrative adjective, two containing *that* as a demonstrative pronoun; two containing *what* as an interrogative pronoun, two containing *what* as an interrogative adjective.

E   *This* is a story about a well-known American millionaire, John D. Rockefeller, and was told by a friend of *his*. *This* friend said that although Rockefeller spent millions to help other people, *he* never liked any expense which was for *himself*.

One day he went to stay at a hotel in New York and asked for the cheapest room *they* had. '*What* is the price of the room?' he asked. The manager told *him*.

'Is that the lowest priced room *you* have? *I* am staying here by *myself* and only need a small room.'

The manager said, '*That* room is the smallest and cheapest *we* have;' and added, 'but why do you choose a poor room like *that*? When *your* son stays here *he* always has *our* most expensive room; *yours* is the cheapest.'

'Yes,' said Rockefeller, 'he has expensive tastes; but *one* can hardly blame him. You see, *his* father is a wealthy man; *mine* isn't.'

Note the words in italics. Say which are adjectives and which are pronouns, and say which kind in each case.

3 Adverbs

Revision. Adverbs go with verbs to tell how an action is done (Adverbs of Manner), when an action is done (Adverbs of Time) or where an action is done (Adverbs of Place). They are often made by adding -*ly* to the adjective; but there are some exceptions. Adverbs generally go after the verb. Phrases that do the work of adverbs are called Adverb Phrases.

Degree Adverbs

You have learned that adverbs go with or 'modify' verbs. But there is one kind of adverb that modifies not only verbs but also adjectives and other adverbs.

Look at these sentences:

Tom did a *very* difficult exercise.

That hat is *too* big for you.

Yes, it is *rather* large.

This book is *more* interesting than that one.

What is the *most* interesting book you have ever read?

All these words are answers to such questions as '... how difficult?' '... how big?' etc., and you will notice that they go with the adjectives *difficult, big*, etc., to tell the degree of 'difficulty', 'bigness', etc.

They are **Adverbs of Degree**, or **Degree Adverbs**.

Some adverbs of degree can modify adverbs, e.g.

Richard ran *very* quickly.

He arrived *too* soon.

He answered the question *quite* easily.

Some adverbs of degree modify verbs, e.g.

I *hardly* know him.

That *nearly* hit me.

I *quite* understand.

Degree adverbs modify verbs, adjectives and other adverbs.

Adverbs of Quantity

There are other adverbs that express 'how often?' These are called **Adverbs of Quantity**, e.g.

I went there only *once* or *twice*.

He comes here *sometimes* (*often*, *daily*, *weekly*, etc.)

I *never* see him now.

Interrogative Adverbs

Some adverbs are used to ask questions. They are **Interrogative Adverbs**, e.g.

Where are you going?

Why did you do that?

When will he come here?

Comparison of Adverbs

You will remember that adjectives have degrees of comparison. (Book 2, pp. 21–26).

You have the same thing with adverbs, but mostly with adverbs of quality, e.g.

Positive	Comparative	Superlative
fast	faster	fastest
early	earlier	earliest
well	better	best
badly	worse	worst

| quickly | more quickly | most quickly |
| happily | more happily | most happily |

or, according to meaning

| quickly | less quickly | least quickly |
| happily | less happily | least happily |

Adverbs and Prepositions

Sometimes the same word may be used as an adverb or as a preposition; it depends on the work the word is doing. If it is governing a noun or a pronoun it will be a preposition, e.g. 'Come and sit *near* me' (Preposition). If it is going with a verb (in which case it won't usually have a noun or a pronoun immediately after it) it is an adverb, e.g. 'The boy sat *near* the door' (Preposition). 'The boy came *near*, when he heard the music' (Adverb).

He went into the room *before* me (Preposition).

I have been to this place *before* (Adverb).

We heard the burglar *inside* the room (Preposition).

It's raining, come *inside* (Adverb).

The bucket went *down* the well (Preposition).

Sit *down* (Adverb).

Exercises

A Here are some degree adverbs: very, too, rather, almost, quite, nearly, more, most, less, terribly, entirely, completely, just, hardly, slightly.

Put one of them to replace each dash in the following sentences and then say whether the degree adverb that you choose is modifying a verb, an adjective or another adverb:

1 This exercise is not _____ difficult.
2 John speaks French _____ well.
3 The explorers _____ died of thirst.
4 He drove the car _____ fast in that busy street.
5 I have _____ finished my work.
6 I think he answered that question _____ cleverly.
7 We are _____ there now.
8 I am _____ sorry to hear that your father is ill.
9 This is one of the _____ difficult questions to answer.
10 What he said was not _____ true.
11 I have _____ forgotten what he said.

12 Your work is _____ important than your games.
13 I know him _____.
14 I _____ know him.
15 Etuk ought to listen _____ and talk _____.

B The words in italics in the following sentences are all adverbs. Say what kind each one is.
  1 Abdul ran down the field *quickly*.
  2 We went to see a friend *yesterday*.
  3 Joseph plays football *well*.
  4 I *quite* agree, he plays *very well*.
  5 We had tea and played games *afterwards*.
  6 *Where* are you going *today*?
  7 I have *often* made that mistake.
  8 *Why* don't you work *more carefully*?
  9 I used to see him *once* or *twice* a week; *now* I *never* see him.
  10 *When* will he learn not to drive his car *so fast*?

C Give the comparative and superlative of the following adverbs. Put the words in sentences:
near, early, *brightly,* pleasantly, well, badly.

*Give two forms (according to meaning) for these.

D Say whether the words in italics are adverbs or prepositions and give reasons for your reply.
  1 The music got louder as the band drew *near*.
  2 I stood *near* Bassey in the crowd.
  3 Your name will be called *before* mine.
  4 You ought to have told me that *before*.
  5 *Inside* that box there are valuable jewels.
  6 I will never go *inside* that house again.
  7 It's very nice to be *outside* when the sun is shining.
  8 He stood *outside* the door, and listened to what was going on *inside*.
  9 The horse ran all *round* the race-course.
  10 The big wheel turned *round* slowly.
  11 If you can't climb *over* the wire fence, get *under* it.
  12 You can go *under*; I'm going to climb *over*.

4   The Present Perfect Tense

Revision. Verbs are words that express an action or a state of being. There is always a verb in the predicate of a sentence and this verb agrees with its subject in number and person. Verbs that take an object are transitive verbs; verbs that don't take an object are intransitive verbs.

The tense of a verb shows (1) the time (present, past or future) when an action takes place, took place or will take place, (2) the completeness or incompleteness of an action. The Present Continuous Tense is used for an action that is still going on. The Simple Present Tense is used for a repeated or habitual action. The Past Continuous Tense is used for an action that was continuing in the past. The Simple Past Tense is used for an action that was completed in the past. Verbs form their negative in two ways: (1) by adding *not* with the infinitive (the method of the Peculiars), (2) by using *do* (*does, did*) *not* and the infinitive (the method of all verbs except the Peculiars).

The parts of verbs that can be a predicate by themselves are called Finites. The parts of verbs that can't be a predicate alone are called Non-Finites. Verbs that form their past tense and past participle by adding *d, ed,* or *t* to the present are called weak, or regular verbs. Verbs that form their past tense and past participle by changing their vowel are called strong or irregular verbs.

TEACHER   (*to one of the pupils*) Come here, John. I want you to help me with this lesson. I am going to ask you to do some simple things and then ask you a few questions. First of all will you open the door, please? (*John does so.*) Now, what have you just done, John?

JOHN   I have opened the door.

TEACHER   Good. I'll write your answers on the blackboard.

> I have opened the door.

(*To Hassan*) What has John just done, Hassan?

HASSAN | He has opened the door.

TEACHER   Now write your name on the blackboard. (*He writes 'John'.*) What have you just done?

JOHN | I have written my name.

TEACHER   What has John done, Rufai?

RUFAI | He has written his name.

TEACHER   And what have I just asked you, Rufai?

RUFAI | You have asked me a question.

TEACHER   John, shake hands with Obi. What have John and Obi just done, Paul?

PAUL | They have shaken hands.

TEACHER   Now, all the class, close your books. What have you all just done?

CLASS | We have closed our books.

TEACHER   Now, look at these sentences on the board. John, put a line under all the verbs. (*John does so.*)

I have opened the door.   We have closed our books.
I have written my name.   You have asked me a question.
He has opened the door.   They have shaken hands.
He has written his name.

Notice that all these verbs have two parts. The first is *have* (or *has*), the second is a non-finite: the non-finite is called the **Past Participle**.

The tense of a verb shows two things (Book 2, p. 40): (1) When an action takes place. (2) Whether the action is finished or not. In the sentences that we have just written down, it is quite clear that the action is finished. When John said, 'I have opened the door', the door was wide open – he had completed the action of opening it. When he said, 'I have written my name', his name was already on the blackboard. But in these cases, we are not really interested in *exactly* when the action took place (unless we add a word like 'just' to show that the action was just finishing at that moment). Our greater interest is in the *present result of the finished action*. We are not wondering at what time in the past, or how long ago, John opened (simple past tense) the door, we are only interested in the fact that at this moment the door is open because of John's action of opening it. Therefore, this tense is a Present Tense. (The verb that is used to show the time of the action is a present tense, have.) But the action is finished (or 'perfected'). So the tense of this verb is called the Present Perfect. All the verbs that I wrote on the blackboard are examples of the Present Perfect Tense.

The Present Perfect Tense is formed by using 'have' ('has') and a past participle.

The Present Perfect Tense is used for an action that is just finished. It is used when we are thinking more about the present result than about the past action.

Exercises

A   Write down the past participles of these verbs:
write, open, know, get, give, break, bring, catch, drive, eat, think, throw, choose, pay, freeze, ride, see, sell, teach, wake.

B   Rewrite the following sentences putting the verb in the Present Perfect Tense.

1 John (*write*) his name.
2 I (*draw*) a picture.
3 Tom (*blow*) out the light.
4 The cat (*drink*) its milk.
5 The tree (*fall*) across the road.
6 John (*give*) his bicycle to his brother.
7 You (*make*) a mistake.
8 The thieves (*take*) the jewels.
9 We (*eat*) our dinner.
10 The train just (*go*).

5 The Present Perfect Tense (2)

The Present Perfect Tense forms its negative by putting *not* after *have* (or *has*). It forms its interrogative by changing the position of the subject and the verb *have*. (You would expect this of course, because *have* is one of the Peculiars.) Here are some examples:

Affirmative.	You *have opened* the door.
Negative.	You *have not* (*haven't*) *opened* the door.
Interrogative.	*Have* you *opened* the door?

Affirmative.	Mary *has been* to the market.
Negative.	Mary *has not* (*hasn't*) *been* to the market.
Interrogative.	*Has* Mary *been* to the market?

Affirmative.	I *have taught* you this before.
Negative.	I *have not* (*haven't*) *taught* you this before.
Interrogative.	*Have* I *taught* you this before?

JOHN   Please, sir, I don't quite understand this Present Perfect Tense.

TEACHER   What's your difficulty, John?

JOHN   Well, sir, I was thinking about these sentences:

I have done English grammar for two years.

Musa has been to Paris three times but he has never been to America.

Have you ever flown to Zimbabwe, Nosa?

I haven't seen Okon since Friday.

It seems to me that all those actions are in the *past*. I did English grammar *last* year and the year before that. (That is *past* time.) Musa went to Paris three times last year. I'm not asking Nosa what he is doing now; I'm asking him if he flew in 1982 or any other time *in the past*. The last time I saw Okon was Friday of *last* week. As all these actions are in the past, it seems funny to me to call that tense the *Present* Perfect.

TEACHER   That's a good point, John. But let us look at your sentences again:

I have done English grammar for two years – UP TO NOW.

Musa has been to Paris three times – UP TO THE PRESENT.

You asked Nosa if he had ever flown to Zimbabwe – UP TO TODAY.

I haven't seen Okon – UP TO THE PRESENT TIME.

You see, in all those sentences there is the idea of NOW, that is, of the PRESENT TIME.

You remember those questions I asked you in the last lesson and the verbs that we marked (see page 15). Well, I am going to ask some more questions rather like them and we will mark these verbs too. I think that may help to clear up your difficulty.

What did you do in the lesson yesterday, John?

JOHN   I | opened | the door.

TEACHER   And what did you do after that?

JOHN   I | wrote | my name.

TEACHER   And what did I do then, Rufai?

RUFAI   You | asked | a question.

TEACHER   And what did John and Obi do a few minutes after, Paul?

PAUL   They | shook | hands.

TEACHER   And what did you all do then?

CLASS   We | closed | our books.

TEACHER   In all those sentences we were thinking of events that happened and were completed in the past, and we used the Simple Past Tense. You probably noticed in my questions just now, the adverbs or adverb phrases that suggest past time, 'yesterday', 'after that', 'then', 'a few minutes after'. You won't find these adverbs or adverb phrases with the Present Perfect Tense. With that tense you will find either no adverb at all, or you will find adverbs or adverb phrases that suggest now, e.g.

'up to now, 'already', 'just', etc. I'll arrange them in two columns, John's original sentences in A and his remarks in B, so that you can compare them easily. I will underline the adverbs or adverb phrases in his remarks.

A	B
Present Perfect	*Simple Past*
I |have done| English grammar for two years.	I |did| grammar last year and the year before that.
Musa |has been| to Paris three times.	He |went| to Paris last March, then in June and in July.
Have |you ever| flown to France?	I'm asking him if he |flew| in 1982.
I |haven't seen| Okon since Friday.	I |didn't see| Okon on Saturday or any other day after Friday of last week.

In examples in the Past Tense there is often a definite time in the past mentioned. In sentences in the Present Perfect Tense the time is often indefinite.

Does that clear up your difficulty, John?

JOHN   Yes, sir, it's quite clear now.

TEACHER   Good. So we can say that the rule is:

The Present Perfect Tense is used for an action that is just finished. It is used when we are thinking more of the present result ('up to now') than about the past action.

The Simple Past Tense is used where we are thinking of an action completed in the past.

Exercises

A   Make the following sentences (a) negative, (b) interrogative:

    1 I have finished the work.

    2 He has written a letter.

    3 The cat has drunk its milk.

4 They have understood the lesson.
5 Noma has gone to the town.
6 I finished the work yesterday.
7 He wrote a letter last week.
8 The cat drank its milk this morning.
9 They understood the lesson.
10 Noma went to the town last week.

B   Supply either the Present Perfect Tense or the Past Tense as required:

1 I just (tell) you the answer.
2 I (tell) you the answer yesterday.
3 Musa never (sail) to America up to the present.
4 John and Rufai just (go) away.
5 She already (answer) the letter.
6 She (answer) it on Tuesday.
7 John and David (go) away five minutes ago.
8 I (read) that book in the summer holidays.
9 The baker (sell) now all his bread.
10 He (sell) the last loaf half an hour ago.

6 The Present Perfect Continuous Tense

You remember of course the Present Continuous Tense and the Past Continuous Tense, e.g.

I *am learning* English grammar now (Present Continuous).

I *was learning* English grammar a year ago (Past Continuous).

Well, you can also have a Present Perfect Continuous Tense, e.g.

I *have been learning* English grammar for two years.

It means 'up to now' and so is *Present* Perfect Continuous.

As you see this tense is made by using the present participle (e.g. *learning*) together with *have* (*has*) *been*.

Mr Thomas *has been teaching* here for twenty years.

Have you seen Sam? *We've been looking* for him all the afternoon.

I've been working on this model engine for six weeks. It's nearly finished now.

It's been raining for two days and it seems it will never stop.

Asmau is a hard worker. *She's been cleaning* the house all morning.

'Is Mary at home now?' 'No, *she's been staying* with her aunt in Accra for the last two months.'

You've been studying the Present Perfect Continuous Tense. I hope you understand it now.

Note the contracted form *we've* = we have: The contracted form *it's* = it has; the form *he's* = he has. Remember that *it's* can also mean it is, *he's* can mean he is, and *she's* can mean she is.

The Present Perfect Continuous Tense is used to express an action that began in the past and is still continuing.

Exercises

A Change the following sentences from Present Continuous Tense to Present Perfect Continuous Tense. Add any words or phrases that you think are necessary:

1 I am learning English grammar at present.
2 The teacher is teaching in this school now.
3 We are looking for Sam.
4 Obi is working on his radio set.
5 It is raining hard.
6 We are peeling cassava.
7 They are living in Ibadan now.
8 The cat is sleeping on the mat.
9 The birds are singing in the forest.
10 Father is writing letters.

B Fill in the blank columns. The first one is done for you.

Present Continuous	Past Continuous	Present Perfect Continuous
1 I am speaking.	I was speaking.	I have been speaking
2 He is working.		
3 She is sewing.		
4 It is raining.		
5 You are learning.		
6 We are studying.		
7 They are digging.		
8 The sun is shining.		

7 Past Perfect Tense

Look for a moment at these two sentences:

Ali learned English. He came to England.

Both these actions took place in the past, so we use the Simple Past Tense, *learned* and *came*.

But suppose we want to show that one of these actions took place before the other one. Suppose we want to say that before he came to England, Ali learned English. Then we use the **Past Perfect Tense** for the action that took place first, and we use the Simple Past Tense for the other action. We say:

Ali *had learned* English before he came to England.

The Past Perfect Tense is formed like the Present Perfect Tense except that instead of using the Present form, *have* (*has*), we use the past form, *had*.

Let us take a few more examples. Suppose we are going to a football match, but we are rather late. We arrive at the football field to find the teams are already playing. Then we would say:

When we reached the field, the game *had started*.

One action (the starting of the game) took place before the other action (our arrival on the football field). The first and earlier action is in the Past Perfect Tense (*had started*), the later action (reached) is in the Simple Past Tense.

Here are some further examples:

Before the fire-engines arrived, the fire *had destroyed* the house.

When I *had finished* my homework I turned on the radio.

Margaret *had* already *got* home before it began to rain.

Paul bought a new dictionary yesterday because he *had lost* his old one.

Before the children came to the party Mary and Tina *had arranged* the room, Mrs Dada *had baked cakes*, and Mr Dada *had bought* a small present for every guest.

The Past Perfect Tense is used to show that one action took place before another action in the past.

Exercises

A Rewrite the following pairs of sentences so that one sentence is in the Past Perfect Tense. Add any words that are necessary:

1 (a) John studied French.   (b) He went to Paris.
2 (a) We arrived at the cinema.   (b) The film started.
3 (a) Kojo ate all the food.   (b) Paul arrived home.
4 (a) The army commander studied all the maps of the district.   (b) He made the attack.
5 (a) The farmer finished clearing the farmland.   (b) He planted some cassava.

B Here is a story. Rewrite it putting all the verbs in brackets into the Past Perfect Tense.

Honest Labi

Chief Fadaka's car just (go) past Labi's beer shop when the driver stopped at the side of the road. This driver once (drop) a large sum of his employer's money in a beer carton which (be) returned to Labi's shop. Labi (find) the money, and (return) it to the driver, who already (hurry) back to Chief Fadaka's house to look for it. He did not even know that he (drop) it in the beer carton, he thought he (leave) it on the table in Chief's house.

'What's the matter, Isiaka?' asked Chief Fadaka.

'Chief, something funny is going on in Labi's shop. Labi's not there, and those men are taking drinks out of the shop and loading them into that big lorry, not the other way round. See how many men there are, and working so fast! Chief, please let us go and alert the police. If thieves carry off Labi's stock that will be the end of his business. He's not even insured – he says he can't afford it.'

By that time, Isiaka (turn) the car round and (drive) towards the nearby police station. After Chief (speak) to a senior officer, a team of policemen was dispatched to Labi's shop. The thieves (finish) loading the lorry, but before they could drive off, the police (surround) them and (arrest) the lot.

On their way home, after they (leave) a policeman on guard at the shop, Chief asked his driver, 'Tell me, Isiaka, why were you so concerned about a beer seller's welfare? He's not your townsman, and you're not even of the same religion.'

'Well, Chief, if that man not (be) honest, I would be in prison now.' And he told Chief Fadaka the story of how he nearly (lose) the money that the Chief (ask) him to deliver for an urgent business transaction.

After he (think) for a minute or two, Chief said, 'You'll be surprised, Isiaka, but if you (lose) that money at that particular time, I would have been in great difficulties. So I too must repay Labi. I shall tell him how to obtain insurance against fire and theft, very cheaply, from the ABZ Insurance Company; and at the next Board meeting of Superior Breweries, of which I am now a director, we shall make him one of our distributors. One good turn deserves another.'

8 The Future Tense

In an earlier lesson (Lesson 10, Book 2) you were told that in the Future Tense we use *shall* with the first person and *will* with all the other persons, e.g.

I *shall* be twelve years old next year.
You *will* be twelve years old next year.
He *will* be twelve years old next year.
We *shall* be twelve years old next year.
They *will* be twelve years old next year.

The negative is formed by adding *not* (both *shall* and *will* are Peculiars).

Will *not* is often shortened to *won't*; shall *not* is often shortened to *shan't*.

I *shall not* (*shan't*) be twelve until next year.
You *will not* (*won't*) be twelve until next year.
He *will not* (*won't*) be twelve until next year.
We *shall not* (*shan't*) be twelve until next year.
They *will not* (*won't*) be twelve until next year.

AFFIRMATIVE   INTERROGATIVE

The interrogative is formed by inversion (See Book 2, p. 57).

Interrogative

Shall I?	Shall we?
Will you?	Will they?
Will he?	

Here are some more examples of the use of *shall* and *will*, *shan't* and *won't*.

Shall we go for a walk?

The sky is black; I think *it will* rain.

Yes, I think *we shall* have a thunderstorm.

No, *we shan't* have rain, the sky is getting clearer.

I hope *it won't* rain; if it does *we shall* have to stay in.

Shall I take an umbrella?

Oh no, *you won't* need an umbrella.

Will you come with us on our walk?

No, *I shall* stay at home and write some letters. Even if it rains *you won't* get very wet.

You're wrong there. I think that if it rains *we shall* get wet through and through.

The Future Tense is used for actions that are going to take place.

In the Future Tense 'I' and 'we' take 'shall' after them. 'He', 'she', 'they' and 'it' and all nouns take 'will' after them.

Exercises

A   Put *shall* or *will* in the blank spaces.

   1 I _____ be fourteen years old next week.
   2 We _____ be late if we don't hurry.
   3 He _____ be thirteen years old on Tuesday.
   4 You _____ be late if you don't hurry.
   5 _____ I open the door for you?
   6 _____ you come to our house for tea?
   7 John _____ come if you ask him.
   8 _____ we ask him to come?
   9 I think we _____ have rain this afternoon.
   10 _____ your friends come and play?

B   Change the following into the future tense. Change words like today, yesterday, etc., into tomorrow, etc., where necessary:

   1 Mr Dada drives the car to the office.
   2 Mr Adamu gives a science lecture.
   3 I learn science from him.
   4 I went to Kumasi yesterday.
   5 John went to Lome yesterday.
   6 I am twelve years old today.
   7 Mary is eleven years old today.
   8 We saw our friends last week.
   9 They stayed with us last Christmas.
   10 It rained yesterday and I got wet. (Begin 'I expect....')

9 The Future Tense (2)

JOHN Please, sir, don't you often get 'I will' as well as 'I shall'? I had a letter from my Uncle Adjei this morning and it said, 'I *will* give you a bicycle for your fourteenth birthday.'

JUNAID Oh yes, sir. My father was angry this morning. He'd just had a bill from the garage for the repair of his car and he said: 'I *won't* pay this bill. The man hasn't done the work properly. *I'll* take the car to another garage.'

(I'll *is the contracted form of* I will.)

GEORGE Yes, and mother said, 'Well, we *won't* discuss it any more just now. Let's have breakfast in peace.'

MARY I was at my Aunt Eno's wedding in Kano in May, and when the clergyman asked Uncle Essiet if he would have Eno to be his wife, I am sure he said 'I *will*' and not 'I shall.'

MARGARET Our radio wouldn't work last night. Daddy worked at it all evening and the last thing that I heard before I went to bed was Daddy saying, 'I *won't* be beaten! I *will* make this radio work, if I stay up all night to do it!'

TEACHER You are all quite right. Every one of those sentences is perfectly correct – and you have started me on one of the most difficult points in English grammar, the use of *shall* and *will*. It would take a great many lessons to explain all about it (and to tell you the truth many English people are not at all sure of the proper use of *shall* and *will*), but I will give you all you need to know at present.

Sometimes the words *shall* and *will* show something else besides a future action. They show something of the feeling that is in the mind of the person using them. An example or two will make clear what I mean. Let's take some of the sentences you mentioned. I'll write them down, side-by-side with the ones we started with.

A	B
I shall be 12 years old	UNCLE ADJEI *I will* give you a bicycle.
tomorrow.	FATHER . *I won't* pay.
We shall have rain.	MOTHER *We won't* discuss
We shall not be taken into	it any more just now.
the University until	DADDY *I will* make this radio work.
1990.	UNCLE ESSIET (at his wedding) *I will*.

Now all those sentences in Column A are just expressing the idea of something that will happen to you in the future, e.g. 'being twelve years old', 'having rain', 'being taken into the University'. You can't do anything about it; you can't change your age or stop the rain even if you wanted to, can you? Those are things that will just happen as time goes by. They all express Simple Future. But was there nothing more than just a future happening in all those other sentences? Wasn't there some *feeling* in the mind of all the speakers? What about Uncle Adjei's words, John?

JOHN   I hope there was something more! I look upon what he said as a definite PROMISE that I am to have a bicycle.

TEACHER   And what about your father, Junaid? Had he any feeling in his mind?

JUNAID   You would have said so if you had heard him! He was angry and quite determined he wasn't going to pay. He was telling us very firmly that it was his INTENTION never to take his car to that garage again.

MARGARET   There was no doubt about my daddy's DETERMINATION when he said, 'I *will* make that radio work.'

TEACHER   And now, Mary, what about your Uncle Essiet's 'I will'?

MARY   Well, I think he was telling all the people there that he was willing to marry Aunt Eno and so he was expressing his WILLINGNESS to marry her.

TEACHER   Yes. In all those cases *I will* meant something more than *I shall*.

'I shall', 'we shall' express Simple Future. The negative is shall not (shan't).

'I will', 'we will' express willingness, intention, promise or determination. The negative is will not (won't).

Exercises

A   What, besides future, is expressed by *I will*?

B   What do you think is expressed by the words in italics in each of the following sentences?

1 I *will* get this exercise right.
2 If you need money I *will* lend you some.
3 You can say what you like, I *won't* help you.
4 He asked me if I would do the work and I said, 'All right, I *will.*'
5 Umaru and I *will* carry your bag for you.
6 We *will* walk to the station and wait for you.
7 We *will* not allow him to open the box until you give permission.
8 I *won't* wash my hands; they're not dirty.
9 If I get the job I *will* work hard.
10 I *will* say what I think, no matter what happens.

10 The Future Tense (3)

I want to return again for a while to *will* and *shall*. You will remember that *I will* expresses willingness, promise, intention or determination, and you will see that when we are talking about people, some feeling like this is always likely to be present. So *I will* and *we will* are used much more often than *I shall*, *we shall*. In fact it is quite likely that *shall* will cease to be used.

The exception to what I have said is in questions, where 'shall I?', 'shall we?' will continue in usage. This is because 'shall I?', 'shall we?' in questions are not used for simple future only, as in:

1) Shall I see you tomorrow?

But also for polite suggestions and for requests, as in:

2) Shall we have a game of netball?

3) Shall I open the window?

In 2) and 3) above, *shall* can never be replaced by *will*.

But in 1) above, simple future, modern usage accepts *will* as well as *shall*, e.g.

Will I see you tomorrow?

How will I recognise your brother?

What about shall/shan't for the other persons? Well, these are not used very often, so they are not of great importance, but you will see them in your reading, so you may as well know them. Here are some examples of the use of the form B:

He shall do the work whether he wants to or not. (DETERMINATION)

You shall have the money I owe you as soon as I get it. (PROMISE)

You've damaged my bicycle. *You shan't* have it again. (DETERMINATION)

Those people want to buy my house, but *they shan't* have it. *I won't* sell it. (DETERMINATION)

They all show determination or promise on the speaker's part.

Perhaps a table with the two forms side by side will show them best.

A Simple Future	B Promise, Determination, Willingness, Intention, Command
I shall	I will
you will	you shall
he will	he shall
we shall	we will
you will	you shall
they will	they shall

As you can see, the forms of the verbs in Column B are the exact opposite of those in Column A.

Thou wilt, thou shalt can still be found in some versions of the Bible, e.g. 'Thou shalt not kill'; 'Thou shalt not steal' are two of the Ten Commandments. But these have become obsolete and are not used in Modern English. We would say instead, 'You must not kill'; 'You must not steal'.

For Simple Future use 'I, we shall'; 'you, he, they will'. For Promise, Determination, Willingness, Intention, Command use 'I, we will'; 'you, he, they shall'.

Going to

We can express future intention in another way, and that is by using **going to**. Look at these examples:

Shehu says he *is going to* work hard next year.

I *am going to* write a letter to my uncle today.

Mr Dikko *is going to* sell his car.

We *are going to* finish our homework after supper.

This is perhaps the commonest way of expressing the future; it saves all difficulty with *shall* and *will*. But remember you can't use 'going to' for Simple Future. You can't say:

'Today is the 14th of April; tomorrow it is going to be the 15th of April.'

It can only be used for intention, or 'strong probability'.

I think I am *going to* have a bad cold

JOHN   Please, sir, will you give us an example of 'strong probability'?

TEACHER   Yes, I am going to do that now. Here are one or two examples:

> I think it *is going to* rain. (That is, 'I think it is very probable that it will rain.')
> I'm afraid the new building *is going to* cost a lot of money.
> We *are going to* have two weeks' holiday soon.

BITRUS   'Mother has bought lots of cakes for our party tomorrow. It's *going to* be a jolly good party.' (Bitrus thinks it is very probable it will be a good party.)

TIMI   'I think I am *going to* have a bad cold and I shan't be able to go to the party.'

So you see **'going to' expresses intention or strong probability**. That last sentence will show the difference between intention and probability. Timi isn't intending to have a cold; I should think he intends *not* to have a cold if he can avoid it, but there's a 'strong probability that he will have one.'

Exercises

A   Without looking at your book write out (a) the forms for Simple Future, (b) the forms for Promise, Determination, etc.

B   Rewrite the following sentences replacing 'shall' or 'will' by 'going to'. There is one sentence that can't be changed. Can you find which one it is?

1 My father will buy me a bicycle for my birthday.

2 Our house will be painted next week.

3 They will leave Freetown tomorrow.

4 We will grow flowers in our garden.

5 If I see him again I shall recognize him.

6 How will you open the box?

7 Won't you have one of these cakes?

8 Won't Mary sing a song for us?

9 Will Paul and Rufai play with us tomorrow?

10 Won't Chuka and Idris play with us tomorrow?

Rewrite the following sentences in the Future Tense (a) using 'shall' or 'will'; (b) using 'going to'. Replace the present or past 'time expressions' by a future time expression.

Example:

He did the work yesterday.

(a) He *will* do the work tomorrow.

(b) He's *going to* do the work tomorrow.

1 I wrote to him last week.

2 My Uncle Adjei gave me a bicycle for my birthday last month.

3 They sold their house last year.

4 Sule worked hard last term.

5 Did Sule work hard last term?

6 What time did you have dinner?

7 Mercy sang a song at the last concert.

8 They built a new school in 1962.

9 Didn't you go to see him yesterday?

10 Didn't Rufai play football on Tuesday?

11 The Future Continuous Tense

The Holidays

JOHN   My father is taking me with him to Abidjan. He has business there and he's taking me along to practise my French.

BALA   Oh, aren't you lucky! I wish I could go to Abidjan. When are you going?

JOHN   Next week. This time next Friday *I shall be getting* into the car that will take us to the airport.

EDET   And my father and I *shall be walking* to the farm.

BISI   And my mother *will be waiting* for me to go and help her in her shop!

IDRIS   Yes, John *will be flying* to Abidjan while I'm coaching my brother who's weak in maths.

EDET   While we are resting at midday, John *will be* ... What *will you be doing*, John?

JOHN   I expect *I shall be having* a meal on the plane.

BALA   I've never been on a plane. What time do you get to Abidjan?

JOHN   If the plane is on time we *shall be landing* on the runway just about the time *you will be eating* your evening meal.

IDRIS   I hope *you won't be feeling* too tired after sitting in one spot all day.

JOHN   *I shall be feeling* too excited to feel tired.

IDRIS EDET BISI BALA   Well, *we shall be thinking* about you next Friday.

JOHN   Thanks. And *I shall be thinking* about you.

In that conversation you had twelve examples of the **Future Continuous Tense**.

The verbs are formed by using the simple future (*I shall, you will*, etc.) with *be* and a present participle. Here are all the forms of the future continuous tense of *to go*.

Affirmative	Interrogative	Negative
I shall be going.	Shall I be going?	I shall not (shan't) be going
You will be going.	Will you be going?	You will not (won't) be going.
He will be going.	Will he be going?	He will not (won't) be going.
We shall be going.	Shall we be going?	We shall not (shan't) be going.
They will be going.	Will they be going?	They will not (won't) be going.

The Future Continuous Tense is used to express an action still continuing in the future.

Exercises

A   Write out the Future Continuous Tense (Affirmative, Interrogative and Negative) of the verb *to write*.

B   Change the following sentences from 1st person (I, we) to 3rd person (he, she, it, they).
   1 I shall be thinking about you.   **2** We shall be playing chess on the train.   **3** I shall be walking to school.   **4** We shan't be getting into the car.   **5** I shan't be feeling excited.

C   Change the following sentences from 2nd or 3rd person into 1st person.
   1 You will be going to school.   **2** He will be feeling excited.
   3 She will be writing a letter.   **4** They won't be playing chess on the train.   **5** They won't be learning grammar.

12 The Future Perfect Tense

A Conversation

MRS EKONG   Uyi, I want you to go to the supermarket before five o'clock. I have this ironing to do. *I shall have done* it in about an hour but I need some tomato puree for cooking.

UYI   Can I go after five o'clock, Mother? I want to listen to a programme on the radio and *it won't have finished* by five o'clock.

MRS EKONG   I'm sorry, but the supermarket *will have closed* by the time the radio programme finishes.

MARY   I'll go, Mother. I don't want to listen to the radio and *I shall have done* my homework before five o'clock.

UYI   Oh, thank you, Mary. *I shan't* even *have begun* my homework at five o'clock, but I'll begin it as soon as supper is over.

MRS EKONG   I hope you will. *We shall have had* supper and *Mary will have washed* the plates by half-past seven, so you can do an hour's work before bed-time. *Will you have done* it all by half-past eight?

UYI   Oh yes, *I shall have finished* everything by eight o'clock. Thank you again, Mary.

FUTURE PERFECT

Now here we have another (and the last) of the tenses, the **Future Perfect Tense**. You can see nine examples of it in that conversation.

The Future Perfect Tense tells us something that will have happened at or before a certain time in the future, e.g.

After five o'clock the owner *will have shut* up his super-market.

Before bed-time Uyi *will have completed* her homework.

This tense is made by using the Simple Future Tense (*I shall, you will*, etc.), together with *have* and the Past Participle.

Here are all the forms of the Future Perfect Tense of the verb *to write*.

Future Perfect Tense

Affirmative	Interrogative	Negative
I shall have written.	Shall I have written?	I shall not (shan't) have written.
You will have written.	Will you have written?	You will not (won't) have written.
He will have written.	Will he have written?	He will not (won't) have written.
We shall have written.	Shall we have written?	We shall not (shan't) have written.
They will have written.	Will they have written?	They will not (won't) have written.

The Future Perfect Tense expresses an action that will have been completed at or before a time in the future.

Here is a table of all the tenses that you have learned.

We will use the verb *walk* to illustrate the tenses.

Present

Simple	Continuous	Perfect
I walk.	I am walking.	I have walked.

Past

Simple	Continuous	Perfect
I walked.	I was walking.	I had walked.

Future

Simple	Continuous	Perfect
I shall (will) walk.	I shall (will) be walking.	I shall (will) have walked.

Exercises

A Write out the Future Perfect Tense (Affirmative, Interrogative and Negative) of the verb *to speak*.

B Rewrite the following sentences putting the verbs that are in brackets into the Future Perfect Tense:
   1 By half-past seven we (eat).
   2 The shop (close) by half-past five.
   3 By the end of the year I (read) three of Ngugi's books.
   4 Before his next visit he (be) to Malaŵi.
   5 I (finish) this work before you go away.
   6 By this time next week you (take) your examination.
   7 We (leave) the house before you get back.
   8 In the year 2000, George Bernard Shaw (be) dead for fifty years.
   9 The game (start) before we reach the field.
  10 I hope it (stop) raining before we have to go.
  11 Before we see you again we (buy) a new car.
  12 He (finish) building the house before the end of the year.
  13 The birds (fly) away before the cat can catch them.
  14 At Christmas Mr Ajai (teach) here for fifteen years.
  15 I hope you (not forget) all about the Future Perfect Tense by the next lesson.

13 Mood

The mood of a verb is the form of a verb that tells the mode (or manner) in which an action is shown.

There are three moods, the Indicative, the Imperative and the Subjunctive (See Book 4).

Indicative Mood

The most frequently used mood, by far, is the Indicative.

The Indicative mood is used to make statements and ask questions, e.g.

Indicative mood

Statements	I heard a noise. The train is coming into the station. The earth moves round the sun.
Questions	Did you hear that noise? Are you Miss Aidoo? Have you understood the lesson?

Imperative Mood

The Imperative mood is used to give commands or make requests.

Imperative mood

Commands	In the name of the law *open* the door! *Come* here and *speak* to me. *Don't* make a noise. *Run!*

With a request we usually add 'please', but this depends on the kind of request, e.g.

Requests	Please *don't* forget to write to me. *Don't* make a noise, please. Please *give* your sister my best wishes. *Let* me help you.

The verbs in *italics* in those sentences are in the Imperative mood.

The Imperative (with one exception) has always the same form as the Simple Present Tense, e.g.

Present Tense	*Imperative*
I take	Take!
I speak	Speak!
You go	Go!
I do	Do!
I don't	Don't!

Please don't shoot

Put your hands up

REQUEST   IMPERATIVE MOOD   COMMAND

The one exception is the verb *to be*: e.g.

Present Tense	Imperative
I am here	Be here!
I am quiet	Be quiet!
You are kind	Be kind!

You will notice that the Imperative form of the verb usually hasn't any subject. Compare these two sentences:

	Subject	Verb	Object
Indicative	I	open	the door.
Imperative	–	Open	the door.

We sometimes say that the subject of the Imperative verb is *you* 'understood'. However, it is sometimes necessary to specify who, among the listeners, is to obey a command, e.g. 'Idris, shut the door'; 'Udo, clean the blackboard.'
In Imperative sentences there is generally no subject.

Exercises

A　Write down the following sentences and put after each whether it is a statement, a question, a command or a request. Add whether the verb is Indicative mood or Imperative mood. Put a question mark (?) where necessary in your answer. The first sentence is done for you.

I will close the door. (STATEMENT. Indicative mood.)

　1　I will close the door.
　2　Close the door.
　3　Don't make a noise.
　4　I promise not to make a noise.
　5　Please be as quiet as you can.
　6　Be here at five o'clock without fail.
　7　I will be here at five o'clock.
　8　Will you be here at five o'clock.
　9　Write your name here, please.
　10　What is your name.

11 I want you to write your name here.

12 Write your name here at once.

13 Take these books away.

14 Have you taken those books away.

15 Don't take those books away.

16 I haven't taken the books away.

17 Write these sentences out carefully.

B   Write how to:
(a) make a fire. (b) get to the school or the station or the post office. (c) clean your shoes.
Use the Imperative in each case.

C   Write sentences telling someone not to:
1 do his work carelessly.
2 come to the class with dirty hands.
3 copy from John's book.
4 leave the door open.
5 kick the dog.
6 eat sweets in the class.
7 forget his book tomorrow.
8 write his exercise in pencil.
9 be silly.
10 frighten the baby.

What mood is used in all these sentences?

14 Voice

Revision. Subjects, Predicates, Objects (Book 1, pp. 45–52).

The word or group of words that we speak about in a sentence is called the Subject.

The Predicate of a sentence is the word or group of words that tells us something about the subject.

The Object of a sentence is a noun (or something that stands for a noun) that tells us the person (or thing) to whom the action of the verb happened.

Verbs that take an object are called Transitive Verbs. Verbs that don't take objects are called Intransitive Verbs.

You may remember that in Book 1 (page 48) you had the sentence:

The dog killed the rat.

and you were told that 'the dog' was the subject of the sentence and 'the rat' was the object. The dog did something; it was the *doer* of the action. The rat had something done to it; it was the *sufferer* or *receiver* of the action.

Very often (as in that sentence) the subject is the doer of the action. But not always. Sometimes we put the sentence the other way round, and the subject is the sufferer of the action. For example I could say: The rat (*subject*) was killed by the dog.

'The rat', which is the subject, didn't do anything; it was the receiver of the action.

When the subject of the sentence is the doer of the action, we say the verb is in the active voice.

When the subject of the sentence is the receiver of the action, we say the verb is in the passive voice.

Here are some more examples:

Active Voice	Passive Voice
Margaret sang a song.	A song was sung by Margaret.
The policeman caught the thief.	The thief was caught by the policeman.
The teacher taught the class.	The class was taught by the teacher.
The boys kicked the ball.	The ball was kicked by the boys.
Did you write this letter?	Was this letter written by you?
Did Shehu answer the question?	Was the question answered by Shehu?
Somebody else did that.	That was done by somebody else.

In all those examples, the subject in the passive sentence is in the singular number; so we used the singular verb *was* and the Past Participle (*sung, caught, written,* etc.) of the verb.

Here are some examples where the subject of the passive sentence is in the plural number; so we use the plural verb *were* and the Past Participle (*eaten, answered, built*).

Active Voice	Passive Voice
The boys ate all the mangoes.	All the mangoes were eaten by the boys.
John answered all the questions.	All the questions were answered by John.
The same man built both those houses.	Both those houses were built by the same man.

Only transitive verbs can be used in the passive voice.

Can't you see why this is? Well, look again at the sentences.

	Subject		Object
ACTIVE	The dog	killed	the rat
	Subject		
PASSIVE	The rat	was killed by the dog	

The subject in the passive sentence is formed by the object in the active one. But if the verb isn't a transitive one there won't be any object!

Exercises

A Say which is the 'doer' and which is the 'receiver' of the action in the following sentences:

1 The cat chased the mouse.
2 Mary hit the ball.
3 The ball was caught by Bitrus.
4 The mouse was chased by the cat.
5 The train was pulled by a powerful engine.
6 A powerful engine pulled the train.
7 The wind blew two big trees down.
8 Two big trees were blown down by the wind.

B Draw four columns like the ones below. Sentences 1 and 2 are done for you to show you the method. Deal with the others in the same way.

No.	Subject	Doer or Receiver?	Voice of Verb
1	The bird	Doer	Active
2	A nest	Receiver	Passive

1 The bird built a nest.
2 A nest was built by the bird.
3 The boys did the exercises.
4 The exercises were done by the boys.
5 The shoes were made by the shoemaker.
6 The shoemaker made the shoes.
7 Mary caught the ball.
8 The ball was caught by Mary.
9 The poem was learned by Ime.
10 We were asked many questions by the teacher.
11 Many people heard the noise of the explosion.
12 The match was won by our team.
13 Ime learned the poem.
14 The noise of the explosion was heard by many people.
15 Mary cooked our food.

C Change the following sentences from active voice to passive voice:
   1 I took the book.
   2 Lateef threw a stone.
   3 Lateef broke the window.
   4 The horses pulled the big wagon.
   5 The thief stole a ring.
   6 Mary cooked the food.
   7 The postman delivered the letters.
   8 Did you write these letters?
   9 Did you cook the food, Mary?
  10 Did you break the window, Lateef?

D Change the following sentences from passive to active voice:
   1 The car was repaired by the mechanic.
   2 The book was taken by Biba.
   3 The dinner was cooked by Mrs Ekong.
   4 The desk was broken by Kasali.
   5 The shots were fired by the soldiers.
   6 These letters were typed by my secretary.
   7 Was this banana grown by you?
   8 Was this ring stolen by the thief?
   9 Were the shots fired by the soldiers?
  10 Were these letters typed by my secretary?

A Good Worker Rebels

Mrs Popo's housegirl was a good worker. She washed clothes well, cleaned the kitchen patiently, and was taught to iron in a very short time. She was also shown how to cook and became expert at it. She was well paid, and Mrs Popo took good care of her. She was good with the children and was loved by all of them. She played games with them, laughed when her hair was pulled by the baby, and washed his nappies so white that they shone in the sun. There was only one thing that she refused to do – she would not polish floors.

'Floors are meant to be walked on,' she argued. 'They will never be polished by me.'

Copy the passage into your exercise books and then put one line under every verb in the active voice and two lines under every verb in the passive voice.

15 Active and Passive Voice (2)

In the last lesson, all the examples of the passive voice were in the past tense, e.g.

A nest *was built* by the bird.

But you can have the passive voice with any of the tenses that you have already learned.

The passive voice as you have seen is made by using a part of the verb *to be* and the Past Participle; and the different tenses in the passive are made by using different parts of the verb *to be*.

Simple Present

Active	Passive
My aunt *sells* cloth.	Cloth *is sold* by my aunt.
Ghanaian farmers *grow* cocoa.	Cocoa *is grown* by Ghanaian farmers.
An electric fire *warms* the room.	The room *is warmed* by an electric fire.
Harmattan *kills* these flowers.	These flowers *are killed* by harmattan.
Cats *eat* mice.	Mice *are eaten* by cats.
Do cats *eat* mice?	*Are* mice *eaten* by cats?
Do farmers *grow* cocoa?	*Is* cocoa *grown* by farmers?
Does my aunt *sell* cloth?	*Is* cloth *sold* by my aunt?

Simple Future

Here are examples of the Simple Future Tense. This time we use *will* (or *shall*) *be* and the Past Participle of the Active verb.

Active	Passive
The cat *will catch* the mouse.	The mouse *will be caught* by the cat.

We *shall finish* the work.	The work *will be finished* by us.
The teacher *will help* us.	We *shall be helped* by the teacher.
The teacher *will correct* our work.	Our work *will be corrected* by the teacher.
I'm afraid the fire *will destroy* those houses.	I'm afraid those houses *will be destroyed* by the fire.
Will the cat *catch* the mouse?	*Will* the mouse *be caught* by the cat?

Note the change from *shall* to *will* in some cases. This is because the subject has changed from 1st person to 3rd person. You also get changes from *will* to *shall*

And here are examples of each of the other tenses.

Present Perfect

The boys *have eaten* some of the cakes.	Some of the cakes *have been eaten* by the boys.
Have the boys *eaten* some of the cakes?	*Have* some of the cakes *been eaten* by the boys?

Past Perfect

The boys *had eaten* some of the cakes before the party began.	Some of the cakes *had been eaten* by the boys before the party began.
Had the boys *eaten* some of the cakes?	*Had* some of the cakes *been eaten* by the boys?

The other tenses are not so commonly used, but here is an example of each:-

Future Perfect

The owner *will have closed* his shop by six o'clock.	The shop *will have been closed* by the owner by six o'clock.

Present Continuous

The farmer *is ploughing* the field.	The field *is being ploughed* by the farmer.

Past Continuous

The farmer *was ploughing* the field.	The field *was being ploughed* by the farmer.

Future Continuous

All next week the workmen *will be painting* our house.	All next week our house *will be being painted* by the workmen.

Omission of the doer of the action

But have you noticed how awkward the passive forms sound? Compare the active and passive examples above and you will see that the active forms are shorter and neater in every case.

In English, the active is the normal form for ordinary use, i.e. we put the doer of the action as the subject of the sentence unless we have a special reason for not doing so. It is when we want to emphasize the result of the action, or draw attention to the receiver or sufferer of the action, that we use the passive form. 'Why are you sad?' 'My dog's been run over.' The death of the dog is what interests us here. Sometimes we have to use the passive because we don't even know the doer of the action, e.g. 'Sir, I can't clean the blackboard because the duster's been removed.'

In those instances where we want to give greater emphasis to the receiver of the action but still want to know the doer, we have to use the complete passive form, e.g. 'Chief Fadaka, your car has been towed away by the police.'

Below are some examples of the passive which sound better with the doer of the action omitted.

Active Voice	*Passive Voice*
People speak English all over the world	English is spoken all over the world.
Do people speak English all over the world?	Is English spoken all over the world?
Somebody built this house in 1500.	This house was built in 1500.
You must answer all the questions on the paper.	All the questions on the paper must be answered.

Must I answer all the questions?	Must all the questions be answered?
They blamed me for something I hadn't done.	I was blamed for something I hadn't done.
Someone printed the book in London.	The book was printed in London.
Did someone print the book in London?	Was the book printed in London?

Here is a summary of all the forms for passive voice, illustrated by the verb *show*.

	Active	Passive
Present Simple	he shows	he is shown
Present Continuous	he is showing	he is being shown
Present Perfect	he has shown	he has been shown
Past Simple	he showed	he was shown
Past Continuous	he was showing	he was being shown
Past Perfect	he had shown	he had been shown
Future Simple	he will show	he will be shown
Future Continuous	he will be showing	he will be being shown
Future Perfect	he will have shown	he will have been shown

Exercises

A Turn the following sentences from active voice to passive voice. Keep the same tense in each case. The doer should be omitted in Nos. 11, 12, 13, 29.

Present Tense

1 The girl rings the bell.
2 Everybody forgets that.
3 The teacher corrects our exercises.
4 Mr Peters coaches the football team.
5 The wind blows the clouds away.
6 Does the wind blow the clouds away?
7 Does the girl ring the bell?

Present Continuous Tense

8 Mary is cooking the meal.

9 Mr Eckersley is teaching that class.

10 The soldiers are defending the city bravely.

11 They are examining the new student now.

12 They are training Kasali to repair cars.

13 They are moving troops to the battle area.

Present Perfect Tense

14 Somebody has broken the window.

15 The cat has caught a mouse.

16 Somebody has left on the electric light all night.

17 Most people have heard this story.

18 Has somebody broken the window?

19 Have the pupils finished the exercises?

Past Continuous Tense

20 Our soldiers were slowly driving back the enemy.

21 The wind was blowing the clouds away.

Past Perfect Tense

22 The shot had frightened the birds.

23 Lightning had struck the house.

Future Tense

24 The postman will deliver the letters.

25 Will the postman deliver the letters?

26 I shall finish the work (*Don't forget the rule about 'shall' and 'will'*)

27 We shall spend the money.

28 Shall we spend the money?

29 People will forget it after a few weeks.

B Turn the following sentences from passive voice to active voice. Keep the same tense in each case.

1 The letters are delivered by the postman.

2 That is forgotten by everybody.

3 The clouds are blown away by the wind.

4 That was forgotten by everybody.

5 The city is being defended bravely by the soldiers.

6 Everything that was needed has been done by George.

16 Sentences. Clauses. Phrases.

Revision (Book 1; pp. 39–40). A group of words that makes complete sense is a sentence. A sentence may make a statement, ask a question, give a command or make a request. A sentence has a finite verb in it; a phrase hasn't. Sentences may be joined together by a conjunction or conjunctions. (Book 1, p. 78).

As you know, a sentence must have a verb in it. A sentence that has only one verb in it is called a **Simple Sentence**. These are simple sentences:

The boy opened the door.	(STATEMENT)
Did the boy open the door?	(QUESTION)
Open the door, please.	(REQUEST)
Open that door at once.	(COMMAND)

A sentence that is made of two or more simple sentences joined by a conjunction, or conjunctions, is called a **Compound Sentence**. These are compound sentences:

The boy opened the door	and	walked into the room.

John works hard	but	Chris is lazy.

Shall I write to him	or	will you telephone?

Mary went to the supermarket	and	Ime helped her mother in

the house,	but	Uyi sat listening to the radio.

Each of the sentences in a compound sentence makes complete sense by itself. The sentences in a compound sentence are all of the same importance. But there are some sentences that are not able to stand by themselves. They contain a verb (as all sentences do) but they make complete sense only when they are used with another sentence. They are called **Clauses**. We will consider them more fully in the next few lessons. Meanwhile remember that:

A clause is a sentence that does not make complete sense by itself. It depends on another sentence for its full meaning.

Exercises

A   What is (a) a simple sentence, (b) a compound sentence, (c) a clause?

B   Make each of the following pairs of simple sentences into a compound one. Omit a word or two where necessary.

1 The boy closed the door. He walked away.
2 Usman works badly. He plays games well.
3 The children finished their lessons. They went home.
4 I like learning grammar. I don't like doing the exercises.
5 We come to school on Friday. We have a holiday on Saturday.

17 Adjective Clauses

An adjective, as you know, tells us something about a noun, e.g.

I like a *good* story.
Eze is a *clever* boy.
Is this your *lost* kitten?
We helped the *shipwrecked* sailors.

But instead of these adjectives, we could use a sentence that does the same work, i.e. that tells us something about the noun. For example:

I like a story | that is good. |

Eze is a boy | who is clever. |

Is this your kitten | which was lost? |

We helped the sailors | who were shipwrecked. |

Each of these sentences (*that is good; who is clever; which was lost; who were shipwrecked*) does the work of an adjective. But none of them makes complete sense by itself. These sentences make complete sense only when they are with the other sentence. So they are clauses. And, because they do the work of an adjective, they are called **Adjective Clauses**. The other sentences on which they depend for their meaning (*I like a story; Eze is a boy; Is this your kitten?; We helped the sailors*) are called **Main Clauses**.

The main clause is the *chief* clause; the adjective clause is a *subordinate* one (that is, it is less important as it depends on another). You can have other kinds of subordinate clauses as

well as adjective ones. We shall meet these later.

A Main Clause and one or more subordinate clauses together make a Complex Sentence.

These are complex sentences. We can 'analyse' them; that is, show them divided into main clauses and subordinate clauses like this:

Main Clause	Subordinate (adjective) Clause
This is the house	that Jack built.
Here is the letter	which I received.
Where is the boy	who looks after the sheep?
They met a hunter	who earned his living by trapping animals.

Sometimes the adjective clause divides the main clause, like this:

The house | that Jack built | has fallen down.

The letter | which I received | is in my pocket.

The boy | who looks after the sheep | is fast asleep.

We analyse those complex sentences like this:

Main Clause	Subordinate Adjective Clause
The house has fallen down ·	that Jack built.
The letter is in my pocket	which I received.
The boy is fast asleep	who looks after the sheep.

The important point to note here is this:

In both groups of sentences, the adjective clause 'that Jack built' has been put next to the noun *house* which it described:

This is the house that Jack built.

The house that Jack built has fallen down.

Similarly, in the next pair of sentences, the adjective clause 'which I received' is put next to the noun *letter* which it described.

The rule therefore is:

The adjective clause must go as near as possible to the noun it describes.

We can analyse complex sentences with adjective clauses more fully like this:

Main Clause	Adjective Clause	Work done by Adjective Clause
This is the house	that Jack built.	qualifies 'house'
Where is the letter	which I received.	qualifies 'letter'
The house has fallen down	that Jack built.	qualifies 'house'
The boy is fast asleep	who looks after the sheep.	qualifies 'boy'

Exercises

A   What is (a) a complex sentence, (b) an adjective clause, (c) a main clause?

B Analyse the following complex sentences, as shown above:

1 This is the bicycle that my uncle gave me.
2 Do you know anyone who wants to buy a motor-bike?
3 Here are the cakes which I bought.
4 Mr Dikko was returning home with the money which he had put in his pocket.
5 The bicycle which my uncle gave me was a birthday present.
6 A motor-bike that won't go is no use.
7 The cakes that I bought have all been eaten.
8 The money which Mr Dikko had drawn from the bank was in his wallet.
9 The house that you see over there is very old.
10 The man who had found the money returned it to Chief Fadaka's driver.

18 Adjective Clauses (2)

You know now what adjective clauses are. Let us see now how they are formed.

Here are two simple sentences:

(a) This is Jack Sprat.   (b) He can't eat any fat.

You can make those two simple sentences into one compound sentence by joining them with the conjunction *and*, like this:

This is Jack Sprat *and* he can't eat any fat.

But here is another way to join them:

This is Jack Sprat who can't eat any fat.

Now we have made the two simple sentences into a complex one. *This is Jack Sprat* is the main clause; *who can't eat any fat* is a subordinate adjective clause. Notice how we made that complex sentence. If you compare it with the compound one you will see that instead of *and* (a conjunction) and *he* (a pronoun) we have used one word, *who*, that does the work of *and* and *he*. The word *who* is a pronoun, because it stands instead of *he*; it is also a conjunction because it joins together (or 'relates') the two sentences. It is called a **Relative Pronoun**.

I can do the work of both of you together

A relative pronoun does the work of a pronoun and a conjunction.

It stands instead of a noun and also joins an adjective clause to another clause in a complex sentence.

The three most commonly used relative pronouns are *who* (used for people), *which* (used for things) and *that* (used for people and things). Here are examples to show you how these relative pronouns join simple sentences together to make complex ones.

Simple sentences.
This is Mrs Sprat.   Mrs Sprat can't eat any lean.

Complex sentence.
This is Mrs Sprat who can't eat any lean.
who = and Mrs Sprat

Simple sentences.
Here are the passengers. They want to travel by this 'plane.

Complex sentence.
Here are the passengers that want to travel by this 'plane.
that = and they

(You can use either *who* or *that.*)

Simple sentences.
I have a book. It teaches English grammar.

Complex sentence:
I have a book which teaches English grammar.
which = and it

(You can use either *which* or *that.*)

But when you are making complex sentences like this, remember to put the adjective clause next to the noun it describes. Here are two examples that are a little different from the ones you have just had.

Simple sentences.
The book teaches me grammar. It is a new one.

Complex sentence.
The book that teaches me grammar is a new one.

Simple sentences.

The man can't eat any fat. The man is called Jack Sprat.

Complex sentence.

The man who can't eat any fat is called Jack Sprat.

TEACHER   Now I will give you two sentences and I want you to write them down and join them by using a relative pronoun. One of the sentences will then be a main clause, the other a subordinate adjective clause. Here are the sentences:

'The hunter earned his living by trapping animals.'

'He could foretell the weather.'

Now, John, read what you have written.

JOHN   The hunter, who could foretell the weather, earned his living by trapping animals.

TEACHER   That, of course, is correct. Which is the adjective clause, Rufai?

RUFAI   Please, sir, mine is different. I have: 'The hunter, who earned his living by trapping animals, could foretell the weather.' Isn't that correct too?

TEACHER   Yes, Rufai. Both are correct. This has brought up an interesting point. We had two sentences about the hunter to join together. The joining has produced two different complex sentences because we were not told which of the two facts about the hunter is the more important. Now, whose sentence do we accept?

JANET   John's is better, because the hunter's work is more important than foretelling the weather.

KOFI   But what if the original story was mainly about the weather? In that case, Rufai's would be the one to choose.

TEACHER   We'll accept both, because it's not important to us which of the two facts becomes the main clause. You won't, as a rule, come up against that problem, because the context, or the rest of the story, will usually help you to pick out the most important sentence, which will become the main clause. What is important is that you should note that in both John's and Rufai's sentences, the adjective clause is next to the noun it describes:

The hunter, who earned his living . . . . or The hunter, who could foretell . . . .

So, tell me the rule again, Rufai.

The adjective clause should go as near as possible to the noun it describes.

Exercises

A **1** What are the three most commonly used relative pronouns?

2 What work is done by a relative pronoun?

3 What is the difference between *who* and *which*?

4 Which relative pronoun can be used for persons and things?

B Make each of these pairs of simple sentences into a complex one by using a relative pronoun.

1 Usman Dikko has a dog. It is called Bonzo.

2 This is the girl. She is going to sing a song.

3 Do you like the bicycle? My Uncle Adjei gave it to me.

4 I have lost the pen. I bought it yesterday.

5 Taba lives in a house. It has a big garden.

6 I have finished the exercises. The teacher told us to do them.

7 These are some mangoes. They grew on my tree.

8 I saw the man. He won the prize.

9 They heard about the battle from a soldier. He had been wounded.

10 We had a friend. He was a famous writer.

11 Usman Dikko's dog chased a car. The dog is called Bonzo.

12 The girl is going to sing a song. She is called Arit.

13 The bicycle was for my birthday. My Uncle Adjei sent it.

14 The pen writes very well. I bought the pen yesterday.

15 Taba went with me to Lagos. Taba lives in that house.

16 The exercises are in this book. The teacher told me to do them.

17 The mangoes grew on my tree. You are eating them.

18 The man won the prize. He is my uncle.

19 The soldier had a wooden leg. He had been wounded in the battle.

20 Our friend wrote a book. He lives in that house.

19 Adverb Clauses: Manner, Time, Place

Revision. Adverbs are words that tell more about verbs. Adverbs of manner tell HOW an action was done; adverbs of time tell WHEN an action was done; adverbs of place tell WHERE an action was done (Book 1, pp. 66–68).

I want you to examine these complex sentences. Each sentence has a main clause and a subordinate clause. So that you can recognise it more easily, the subordinate clause is printed in italics.

Manner

John did that work *as it should be done.*
The man ran *as if wolves were chasing him.*
Answer the questions *as you have been taught.*
He fought *as a brave man should fight.*

It is quite clear that these clauses are not like the ones in Lesson 17. They are not describing a noun; they are telling more about the verbs *did*, *ran*, *answer*, and *fought*, i.e. they are doing the work of adverbs. They are **Adverb Clauses**.

'How did John do the work?' 'How did the man run?' 'How must you answer the questions?' 'How did he fight?'

They are doing the work of Adverbs of Manner, so they are **Adverb Clauses of Manner**.

Time

Here are some more adverb clauses:

The thief ran away *when he saw the policeman.*
When I have finished my work, I shall go out to play.
My tooth stopped aching *when the dentist came in.*
A cold wind sprang up, *just as the sun was setting.*
She decided to wait *until the train arrived.*

In these sentences the subordinate clause tells us when the thief ran away, when I shall go out to play, when the tooth stopped aching, when the cold wind sprang up, and up to what time she decided to wait.

They are **Adverb Clauses of Time**.

Place

Let us now examine another group of sentences:

Mary put the meat *where the cat couldn't reach it*.

The sailors went *where they expected to find the treasure*.

Where there are flowers, you will generally find bees.

Wherever Usman goes, Bonzo is sure to go.

Where did Mary put the meat? Where did the sailors go? In what place will you generally find bees? Where is Bonzo sure to go?

These clauses are **Adverb Clauses of Place**.

An Adverb Clause is one that does the work of an Adverb.

Clauses that tell 'how' an action is done are Adverb Clauses of Manner; those that tell 'when' an action is done are Adverb Clauses of Time; those that tell 'where' an action is done are Adverb Clauses of Place.

Complex sentences containing adverb clauses can be analysed like this:

Main Clause	Adverb Clause	Kind of Adverb Clause	Work done by Adverb Clause
John did that work	as it should be done.	Manner	modifying the verb 'did'
I shall go out to play	when I have finished my work	Time	modifying the verb 'shall go'
Mary put the meat	where the cat couldn't reach it.	Place	modifying the verb 'put'

Adverbs are said to 'modify' or tell more about verbs.

Exercises

A What work does an Adverb Clause do? What kinds of Adverb Clauses do you know? Say what each kind does.

B Analyse the following complex sentences in the style shown on page 66:

  1 When we arrived at the football field the game had started.

  2 Chris left dirty footmarks wherever he went.

  3 Kick the ball as hard as Chuka did.

  4 Don't handle those cups and saucers as if they were made of iron.

  5 I am standing where I can see the game.

  6 You can't come into this room while we are having a lesson.

  7 As soon as the boys came into the room the noise started.

  8 Use the paint-brush as I showed you yesterday.

  9 Everywhere I looked there were dirty footmarks.

  10 Our friends had arrived before we got home.

20 Noun Clauses

Now we come to the last kind of clause, **the Noun Clause**. You can, no doubt, guess by now that a noun clause will be one doing the work of a noun. A noun is sometimes the object of a verb (Book 1, page 48–50).

Here are some sentences where the object is a noun:

	Object
Fred dreamed	*a dream.*
I know	*arithmetic.*
Mary said	*a few words.*

Now instead of using nouns for the objects of those verbs we'll use a clause.

	Object
Fred dreamed	*that he was travelling to the moon.*
I know	*that two and two make four.*
Mary said	*that she was wearing a new dress.*

These clauses are objects of verbs. Test them if you like. You remember the test for objects, don't you? (Book 1, page 49) You put the question word 'what?' after the verb, e.g.

'dreamed what?' . . . And the answer comes:

'that he was travelling to the moon.' Then that clause is the object of the verb *dreamed*.

'I know – what?' . . . *Answer*: 'that two and two make four.'

Those clauses, then, are doing the work of a noun. They are **Noun Clauses**.

Almost every noun clause you meet will be the object of a
transitive verb, usually a verb like *say, think, believe*, etc.

But you will remember that nouns are also sometimes the
subject of a verb; and therefore sometimes a noun clause is the
subject of a verb.

Here are two simple sentences each with a noun for the
subject.

Subject	
Your work	seems very difficult.
The prisoner's escape	is a complete mystery.

Now, instead of the noun *work* and the noun *escape* we will
put a clause that is doing exactly the same work, i.e. acting as
subject of the verb *seems* and the subject of the verb *is*:

Subject	
What you are doing	seems very difficult.
How the prisoner escaped	is a complete mystery.

TEACHER   Tina, what work is done by the clauses: *What you are
doing* and *How the prisoner escaped?*
TINA   The work of a noun; each of them is the subject of a verb.
TEACHER   Good. And how do you know they are clauses, John?
JOHN   Because they have a verb in them – so they are not
phrases. They don't make complete sense by themselves so
they are not sentences. They form part of a complex sentence. They are noun clauses.
TEACHER   We can analyse these complex sentences like this:

Main Clause	Noun Clause	Work done by Noun Clause
Fred dreamed	that he was travelling to the moon.	object of 'dreamed'

I know	that two and two make four.	object of 'know'
Mary said	that she was wearing a new dress.	object of 'said'
is very difficult	What you are doing	subject of 'is very difficult'
is a complete mystery	How the prisoner escaped	subject of 'is a complete mystery'

A Clause that does the work of a noun in a sentence is a Noun Clause.

A Noun Clause is generally the object or the subject of a verb.

Exercises

A　What does a noun clause do?

B　Analyse these complex sentences as shown on page 90–91:

1　Usman said he was taking Bonzo for a walk.
2　Samuel hopes that the teacher won't ask him a question.
3　I believe that you are telling the truth.
4　I have forgotten what your name is.
5　The pupils said that the questions were too difficult.
6　'They are quite easy,' replied the teacher.
7　Show me how I must do these exercises.
8　What you said was quite true.
9　I asked the porter if the train had gone.
10　Why I made that mistake I don't know.

C　Complete these sentences by adding a clause:

1　Yussuf said that . . .
2　I believe that . . . .
3　He doesn't think that . . .
4　Ruth believes that . . .
5　Wenike promised that . . .
6　I am very much afraid that . . .
7　Does John know that . . .
8　Bello heard one day that . . .
9　I see that . . .
10　I certainly hope that . . .

What are all the clauses that you have added?

21 Direct and Indirect Speech

TEACHER   The following sentences were spoken by Kassim at different times. I want five of you to tell me, in your own words, what he said, beginning 'Kassim said . . .' or 'He said . . .':

    1   I am in the classroom, and I am writing my exercise.

    2   I have a pen in my hand.

    3   My books are on my desk.

    4   I come to school at eight o'clock

    5   When I have finished my work I shall go out and play.

Now, who'll start?

CELIA   Kassim said that he was in the classroom and was writing his exercise.

ITA   He said that he had a pen in his hand.

HAMZAT   He said that his books were on his desk.

ADA   He said that he came to school at eight o'clock.

GOGO   He said that when he had finished his work he would go out and play.

In that conversation you had a number of sentences expressed in two ways:

    1   By Kassim.

    2   By the pupils who reported what Kassim said.

When you read Kassim's words you have the exact words of the speaker.

Kassim's sentences are **Direct Speech**.

When you read the words of the other pupils you have a different form. You don't get the words exactly as Kassim said them but as they were reported, indirectly, by another speaker. It is no longer Kassim saying 'I', but someone speaking about Kassim and so saying 'he'. Moreover, it is not Kassim speaking in the *present* time, but someone else, telling you what Kassim said in the *past*. The pupils' sentences are **Indirect Speech**.

Let us put some of those sentences side by side and see the differences between Direct Speech and Indirect Speech.

Direct	Indirect
	The pupil said that:
I am in the classroom and am writing.	he was in the classroom and was writing.
I have a pencil.	he had a pencil.
I come to school at eight o'clock.	he came to school at eight o'clock.
I shall go out and play.	he would go out and play.

Here are some further examples:

Direct	Indirect
John said, 'I am going to London with my father.'	John said that he was going to London with his father.
Zainab said, 'Our train will arrive in five minutes.'	Zainab said that their train would arrive in five minutes.
Felicia said, 'My sister speaks French well.'	Felicia said that her sister spoke French well.
Mary said, 'I hope it won't rain'.	Mary said that she hoped it wouldn't rain.
Kwame said, 'I am a pupil and I have learned grammar for three years.'	Kwame said that he was a pupil and had learned grammar for three years.

I will win the race

DIRECT

He said he would win the race

INDIRECT

You will notice that:

1 When a sentence changes from Direct Speech to Indirect Speech, it is introduced by a verb in the past tense: *He said that*

2 All the verbs are changed from present tense to past tense. The Present Perfect Tense is changed to the Past Perfect Tense. However, modern usage does not carry this change of tense right through in certain circumstances. Galileo said, 'The world is round.' Although he said it hundreds of years ago, the universal truth he discovered then has not changed up until today. Therefore, he can be correctly reported thus: *Galileo said that the world is round.* If, in the 21st century, some new scientific instrument should convince us that the world is not really round after all, but that it is 'ovoid' or 'rotoid' (or some such name), we would then have to say: *Galileo said that the world was round.*

Similarly, when reporting something very recently said, about a situation which has not changed, we can correctly say:

He said he always reads at night. (He still has a habit of reading at night.)

What about this: 'I missed that programme because my hostess has no TV set. She says she never watches television.' Both verbs are, correctly, in the present tense here. 'She says ...' is treated like her unchanging opinion, rather than something said at one particular time. In a parallel situation, we could also have said, as an alternative to the example above: *He says he always reads at night.*

3 Pronouns and possessive adjectives in the 1st person are changed to pronouns and possessive adjectives in the 3rd person; i.e. 'my' and 'our' change to 'his' ('her') and 'their.'

4 In Direct Speech you have quotation marks ('...'). In Indirect Speech you do not.

Exercises

A What is the difference between Direct Speech and Indirect Speech? Which has quotation marks, Direct Speech or Indirect Speech?

B When you change sentences from Direct Speech to Indirect Speech what happens to (a) verbs in the Simple Present Tense, (b) verbs in the Present Perfect Tense, (c) pronouns and possessive adjectives in the 1st person?

C Change the following from Direct Speech to Indirect Speech. Begin He (She, They, Bello, Mary, The teacher, etc.) said that:

1 'I like my dog, Bonzo.'
2 'I am going to the party with my brother.'
3 'We have plenty of time to do our work.'
4 'George has written me a long letter.'
5 'We are very tired.'
6 'You sing very nicely, Arit.'
7 'I am giving a prize for the best homework.'
8 'I am French but I have learned English at school.' .
9 'I will take you to my house.'
10 'You can come with us if you like.'
11 'If it rains I shall get wet.'
12 'I am going to give you an exercise on Indirect Speech. It will not be easy, but if you are thoughtful you can do it, as I have given you all the information you need. You can look in your book if you wish, but I don't want you to ask anyone to help you.'